Up in tl Attic

Written by Sasha Morton

Illustrated by Valentina Bandera

RISING ★ STARS

Nan has a lot of stuff in her attic.

lamp

bugs

clock

box

dolls

Zak and Yazz are on a quest!

Nan spots the mess and dust.

She yells at Zak and Yazz.

It must all go back up!

They zip up the bags.

Talk about the story

Ask your child these questions:

1 Who was up in the attic?

2 Which items in the attic belonged to Yazz?

3 What was wrong with Zak's squid?

4 Why wasn't Nan happy about Zak and Yazz taking things out of the attic?

5 Have you ever been in an attic? Was it like the one in the story?

6 How do you feel when you find something you thought was lost?

Can your child retell the story in their own words?